A Child's Place

HARCOURT BRACE SOCIAL STUDIES

FLORIDA Daily Reading Support
for Social Studies

Harcourt
SCHOOL PUBLISHERS

Orlando   Austin   New York   San Diego   Toronto   London

Visit *The Learning Site!*
www.harcourtschool.com

For permission to reprint copyrighted material, grateful acknowledgment is made to the following sources:

Agencia Literaria Latinoamericana: "Son del pueblo trabajador" from *Caminito del monte* by David Chericián. Published by Editorial Gente Nueva.

Hampton-Brown Books: "Chant of the Working People," translated by Juan Quintana from *A Chorus of Cultures: Developing Literacy Through Multicultural Poetry* by Alma Flor Ada, Violet J. Harris, and Lee Bennett Hopkins. Translation copyright © 1993 by Hampton-Brown Books.

Printed in the United States of America

ISBN 0-15-341047-7

1 2 3 4 5 6 7 8 9 10   082   14 13 12 11 10 09 08 07 06 05

Contents

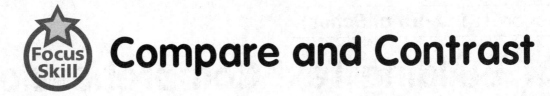

Compare and Contrast

Think about two different people you know. Tell how
the people are alike and how they are different.

REMEMBER

- Think about how the two people are alike.

- Think about how the two people are different.

People I Know	
Alike	**Different**

LA.A.2.1.1(1.4) identifies similarities and differences between two texts (for example, in topics, characters, and
problems).
LA.A.2.1.3(1.1) reads for information used in performing tasks (for example, directions, graphs, charts, signs,
captions).

Name _____ Date _____

Building Text Comprehension
Compare and Contrast

Read the paragraph. As you read, think about how you
get to school. Then fill in the table on the next page.
Compare the way you get to school with ways other
children get to school.

Children go to school to learn.
They get to school in many ways.
Some children walk. Others
ride the bus. Some children ride
to school with their parents.

(continued)

LA.A.2.1.1(1.4) identifies similarities and differences between two texts (for example, in topics, characters, and problems).
LA.A.2.1.3(1.1) reads for information used in performing tasks (for example, directions, graphs, charts, signs, captions).

Name _____ Date _____

Fill in the table.

Compare and Contrast

Alike	Different

LA.A.2.1.1(1.4) identifies similarities and differences between two texts (for example, in topics, characters, and problems).
LA.B.2.1.1(1.3) writes questions or makes notes about familiar topics, stories, or new experiences.

Lesson 2: My Classroom

Building Fluency

Part A. Practice reading the words aloud.

Vocabulary Words	Additional Words
school teacher friends	classroom learn

Part B. First, practice reading aloud the phrases.

Then, practice reading aloud the sentences.

1 I like / to sit / in my classroom.

2 I learn / many things / at school.

3 My teacher / helps me write.

4 I go / to school / with my friends.

5 I wrote / a letter / in my classroom.

6 I drew / a picture / of my friends.

(continued)

LA.A.1.1.4(1.1) uses a variety of strategies to comprehend text (for example, retelling stories in correct sequence, recalling details, rereading).
LA.A.2.1.2(1.2) reads aloud familiar stories, poems, or passages with a beginning degree of fluency and expression.

Part C. Read aloud the passage below three times. Try to improve your reading each time. Record your best time on the lines below.

My classroom is where I learn at school. I read in my classroom. I write there, too. My teacher helps me learn.

Number of words	22
My best time	_____
Words per minute	_____

LA.A.1.1.4(1.1) uses a variety of strategies to comprehend text (for example, retelling stories in correct sequence, recalling details, rereading).
LA.A.2.1.2(1.2) reads aloud familiar stories, poems, or passages with a beginning degree of fluency and expression.

Lesson 3: School Workers

Reading Biographies

Read the paragraph. Then write a sentence about how Mary McLeod Bethune shows the character trait **citizenship**.

Mary McLeod Bethune
Character Trait: Citizenship

Mary McLeod Bethune opened a school in Daytona Beach, Florida. She wanted to give African American children a chance to learn. Most of the children in her school were girls.

_____

- -

_____

- -

_____

- -

_____

- -

_____

- -

_____

LA.A.2.1.1(1.2) uses specific details and information from a text to answer literal questions.
LA.A.2.1.1(1.3) makes inferences based on text and prior knowledge (for example, regarding a character's traits, feelings, or actions).

© Harcourt

Name _____   Date _____

Reading Primary Sources

Long ago, children used hornbooks to learn to read. A hornbook was a flat board with a handle. On the board was the lesson paper. A sheet of clear horn, like plastic, kept the paper clean. Look at the picture of the hornbook.

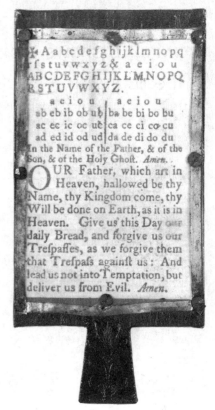

1 What is at the top of the hornbook?

_____

- -

_____

2 Why do you think vowels are listed on the hornbook?

_____

- -

_____

3 What do you use to learn to read?

_____

- -

_____

LA.A.2.1.1(1.1) knows the main idea or theme and supporting details of a story or informational piece.
LA.A.2.1.1(1.2) uses specific details and information from a text to answer literal questions.

Use with Unit 1, Lesson 4.   **7**   **Reading Support for Social Studies**

Lesson 5: We Help One Another

Reading Drawings

Children also work to read and learn. Look at the drawing. It shows the locations of where things are in the library.

Our Library

1 Circle the librarian.

2 Mark an X on the desk where a child could work alone.

3 Color the table where children could work on computers together.

LA.A.2.1.3(1.1) reads for information used in performing tasks (for example, directions, graphs, charts, signs, captions).

© Harcourt

Name _____ Date _____

Building Vocabulary

Read each class rule. Then draw a picture for each rule.

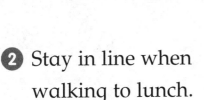 Raise your hand
to speak.

2 Stay in line when
walking to lunch.

3 Do not talk when
the teacher
is talking.

(continued)

LA.A.1.1.2(1.5) uses context clues to construct meaning (meaning cues) (for example, illustrations, knowledge of the story and topic).
LA.A.1.1.3(1.3) uses resources and references (for example, illustrations, knowledge of the story and topic) beginning dictionaries, available technology to build upon word meanings.

© Harcourt

4 Be quiet in the library.

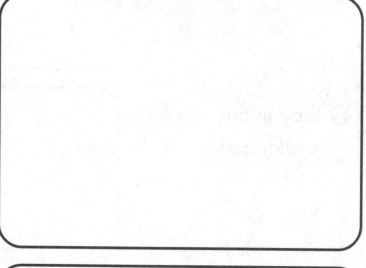

5 Throw garbage in trash cans.

6 Don't chew gum.

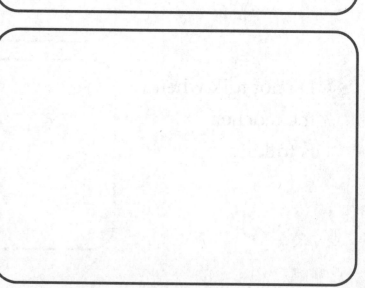

LA.A.1.1.2(1.5) uses context clues to construct meaning (meaning cues) (for example, illustrations, knowledge of the story and topic).

LA.A.1.1.3(1.3) uses resources and references (for example, illustrations, knowledge of the story and topic) beginning dictionaries, available technology to build upon word meanings.

© Harcourt

FCAT Test Prep

Read the passage "The Oldest Wooden Schoolhouse" before answering Numbers 1 through 5. Circle the letter of the best answer.

The Oldest Wooden Schoolhouse

What were schools like in the United States a long time ago? The Oldest Wooden Schoolhouse is in St. Augustine, Florida. It is more than 200 years old. The teacher lived upstairs. The classes were held downstairs.

The old schoolhouse is made of cedar and cypress wood. It was built using wooden pegs and handmade nails. The kitchen is away from the main building. This protects the schoolhouse from fire.

In 1937 a huge chain was attached to the small building to hold it down. The people of St. Augustine were afraid it might blow away in a strong wind.

GO ON ▶

Name _____ Date _____

Now answer Numbers 1 through 5. Base your answers on the passage "The Oldest Wooden Schoolhouse."

1 The Oldest Wooden Schoolhouse is more than

A 100 years old.

B 300 years old.

C 200 years old.

D 500 years old.

2 What building materials were NOT used?

F stone

G handmade nails

H cedar

I cypress

3 In 1937, what was attached to the building?

A a chain

B wood

C a peg

D a chalkboard

4 What does the word <u>handmade</u> mean?

F made of cedar

G made by hand

H easily made

I made of cypress

5 List one interesting fact about the Oldest Wooden Schoolhouse.

READ
THINK
EXPLAIN

_____

- -

_____

- -

_____

STOP

Name _____ Date _____

Sequence

Read the paragraph. Then complete the chart on the next page.

Tami gets ready for school the same way every day. First, she gets dressed. Next, she eats breakfast. Then, she cleans up. Last, Tami brushes her teeth.

REMEMBER

- Look for sequence words such as first, next, then, and last.

- Write the steps in the boxes in the correct order.

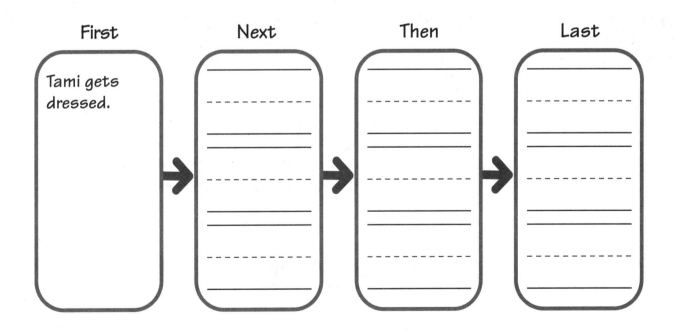

First

Tami gets dressed.

Next

Then

Last

LA.A.1.1.4(1.1) uses a variety of strategies to comprehend text (for example, retelling stories in correct sequence, recalling details, rereading).
LA.A.2.1.3(1.1) reads for information used in performing tasks (for example, directions, graphs, charts, signs, captions).

© Harcourt

Lesson 1: Welcome Home

Building Text Comprehension
Sequence

Focus Skill

Read the paragraph. Then fill in the sequence chart on the next page. Tell how Margie gets to school.

I live on Ralph Road. Every day I walk to school. My home is not far from the school. First, I walk down Sunshine Road. Next, I turn right on Alligator Street. A crossing guard stops the traffic. She makes sure I am safe. Then I cross the street. At last, I turn left into the school yard.

(continued)

LA.A.1.1.4(1.1) uses a variety of strategies to comprehend text (for example, retelling stories in correct sequence, recalling details, rereading).
LA.A.2.1.3(1.1) reads for information used in performing tasks (for example, directions, graphs, charts, signs, captions).

Name _____ Date _____

Fill in the chart.

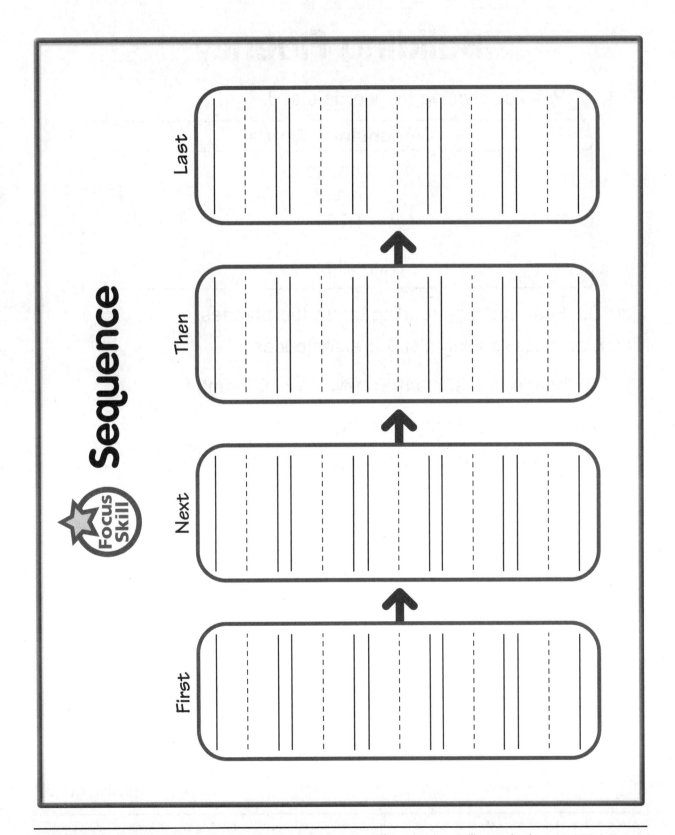

LA.A.1.1.4(1.1) uses a variety of strategies to comprehend text (for example, retelling stories in correct sequence, recalling details, rereading).

Lesson 2: *The Leaving Morning*

Building Fluency

Part A. Practice reading the words aloud.

Vocabulary Words
change
misty
pane
deli
apartment

Part B. First, practice reading aloud the phrases.

Then, practice reading aloud the sentences.

1 A change is / something new / or different.

2 We left / on a misty morning.

3 The window pane / was cold.

4 We drank / hot cocoa / at the deli.

5 We said good-bye / to our apartment.

(continued)

LA.A.1.1.4(1.1) uses a variety of strategies to comprehend text (for example, retelling stories in correct sequence, recalling details, rereading).
LA.A.2.1.2(1.2) reads aloud familiar stories, poems, or passages with a beginning degree of fluency and expression.

© Harcourt

Part C. The passage below is from <u>The Leaving</u> <u>Morning</u> by Angela Johnson. Read aloud the passage three times. Try to improve your reading each time. Record your best time on the lines below.

We sat on the steps and watched the movers. They had blue moving clothes on and made bumping noises on the stairs. There were lots of whistles and "Watch out, kids."

Number of words	**31**
	_____
My best time	_____
	_____
	_____
Words per minute	_____

LA.A.1.1.4(1.1) uses a variety of strategies to comprehend text (for example, retelling stories in correct sequence, recalling details, rereading).
LA.A.2.1.2(1.2) reads aloud familiar stories, poems, or passages with a beginning degree of fluency and expression.

© Harcourt

Name _____ Date _____

Reading Charts and Graphs

This bar graph shows how the children in Ms. Brown's class used their money. Use the information to answer the questions.

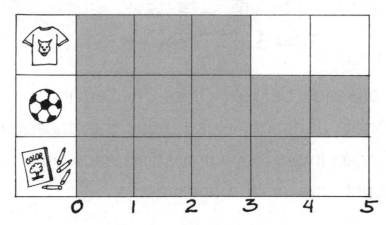

1 Which choice did the most children make?

_____

- -

_____

2 Which choice did the fewest children make?

_____

- -

_____

3 Which choice would you make?

_____

- -

_____

LA.A.2.1.3(1.1) reads for information used in performing tasks (for example, directions, graphs, charts, signs, captions).

Lesson 4: Families Long Ago

Building Vocabulary

Read the sentences.

People <u>celebrate</u> many special times.

A <u>holiday</u> is a special day.

Draw a picture of something you use to celebrate
a holiday.

LA.A.1.1.2(1.5) use context clues to construct meaning (meaning cues) (for example, illustrations, knowledge of the story and topic).
LA.A.1.1.3(1.3) uses resources and references (for example, illustrations, knowledge of the story and topic) beginning dictionaries, available technology to build upon word meanings.

FCAT Test Prep

Read the passage "Tony's Tough Choice" before answering Numbers 1 through 5. Circle the letter of the best answer.

Tony's Tough Choice

Tony gets an allowance for helping around the house. He has worked hard and saved $15.00. Tony has a choice to make. What will he buy with his money?

Tony wants a football that costs $10.00. He also wants a toy car that costs $8.00. He does not have enough money to buy both. Soon it will his sister's birthday. He may use some of his money to buy her a gift. He thinks very carefully about the best way to spend his money.

Tony decides to buy the toy car. He uses some of his money to buy his sister a birthday gift. Tony does not spend all of his money. He decides to save some. Maybe he will buy the football next time.

Go On ▶

© Harcourt

Name _____ Date _____

FCAT

Now answer Numbers 1 through 5. Base your answers
on the passage "Tony's Tough Choice."

1 **How much money does Tony have?**

   A $15.00

   B $3.00

   C $8.00

   D $10.00

2 **What is NOT a choice that Tony has about how to spend his money?**

   F buy a football

   G buy a toy car

   H buy his sister a birthday gift

   I buy a basketball

3 **What does Tony give up when he makes his choice?**

   A the toy car

   B his sister's birthday gift

   C the football

   D saving his money

4 **How do you know that Tony uses his money carefully?**

   F He spends all his money.

   G He saves his money.

   H He buys his sister a birthday gift.

   I He wants new toys.

5 **Write a sentence telling what choice you would make if you were Tony.**

READ
THINK
EXPLAIN

_____

- -

_____

_____

- -

_____

© Harcourt

Name _____ Date _____

Prior Knowledge

Get ready to interview a person in your community. First, write what you know about the person in column one. Next, write questions that tell what you want to know in column two. Then, interview the person. After your interview, write what you learned in column three.

REMEMBER

• Use what you already know to help you think of questions.

• Ask the questions in column two during the interview.

K-W-L Chart		
What I Know	What I Want to Know	What I Learned

LA.A.1.1.1(1.1) uses prior knowledge, illustrations, and text to make predictions.
LA.A.1.1.4(1.1) uses a variety of strategies to comprehend text (for example, retelling stories in correct sequence, recalling details, rereading).
LA.A.2.1.3(1.1) reads for information used in performing tasks (for example, directions, graphs, charts, signs, captions).

Name _____ Date _____

 # Building Text Comprehension
Prior Knowledge

What rules and laws are there for bicycle riders? In the K-W-L chart, write what you know and what you want to know. Then read the paragraph about bicycle laws. Use what you learned to fill in the chart on the next page.

Every state has laws, or rules, for bicycle riders. State leaders make laws so that citizens stay safe. When you ride your bicycle, be sure to follow these laws.

The law says bicycle riders must have the proper safety gear. Children under 16 years old must wear a bicycle helmet with a strap. For traveling at night, a bicycle must have a white light on the front. It must also have red reflectors on the back.

Remember to follow these laws for safe biking!

(continued)

LA.A.1.1.1(1.1) uses prior knowledge, illustrations, and text to make predictions.
LA.A.1.1.4(1.1) uses a variety of strategies to comprehend text (for example, retelling stories in correct sequence, recalling details, rereading).
LA.A.2.1.3(1.1) reads for information used in performing tasks (for example, directions, graphs, charts, signs, captions).

Name _____ Date _____

Fill in the chart.

Prior Knowledge

K-W-L Chart		
What I Know	What I Want to Know	What I Learned

LA.A.1.1.1(1.1) uses prior knowledge, illustrations, and text to make predictions.
LA.A.2.1.3(1.1) reads for information used in performing tasks (for example, directions, graphs, charts, signs, captions).

Name _____ Date _____

Reading Time Lines

Use the time line to answer the questions. See how the post office handles mail.

The letters go to the post office.	The letters are sorted.	A mail carrier delivers the letters.

1 What happens first on the time line?

_____

- -

_____

2 Who delivers the letters?

_____

- -

_____

3 Do the letters get delivered before or after they are sorted?

_____

- -

_____

LA.A.1.1.4(1.1) uses a variety of strategies to comprehend text (for example, retelling stories in correct sequence, recalling details, rereading).
LA.A.2.1.3(1.1) reads for information used in performing tasks (for example, directions, graphs, charts, signs, captions).

Lesson 3: Community Leaders

Reading Biographies

Read the paragraphs. Then write a sentence about how
Lawton Chiles shows the character trait **responsibility**.

Lawton Chiles
Character Trait: Responsibility

In 1970 Lawton Chiles wanted to be
one of Florida's leaders. He walked
more than 1,000 miles across the state
to meet Florida citizens. He became
known as "Walkin' Lawton."

Lawton Chiles was a Florida leader
for 18 years. He worked to pass laws
that would help Florida's children. In
1990 he became governor of Florida. As governor, he
worked to get better health care and education for
children. Lawton Chiles was a leader who cared
about the youngest citizens of Florida.

_____

- -

_____

- -

_____

LA.A.2.1.1(1.2) uses specific details and information from a text to answer literal questions.
LA.A.2.1.1(1.3) makes inferences based on text and prior knowledge (for example, regarding a character's traits, feelings, or actions).

Lesson 4: A Community Changes

Building Fluency

Part A. Practice reading the words aloud.

Vocabulary Words
college
Show and Tell
workers
grew

Part B. First, practice reading aloud the phrases. Then, practice reading aloud the sentences.

1 My community changed / when it built / a college.

2 I will bring my book / to Show and Tell.

3 Workers cleared the land / and built the college.

4 The community grew / when people started / moving here.

(continued)

LA.A.1.1.4(1.1) uses a variety of strategies to comprehend text (for example, retelling stories in correct sequence, recalling details, rereading).
LA.A.2.1.2(1.2) reads aloud familiar stories, poems, or passages with a beginning degree of fluency and expression.

Part C. Read aloud the passage below three times.
Try to improve your reading each time. Record your
best time on the lines below.

My community has changed a lot. My dad told
me it changed when a college was built here. He
showed me pictures. I put the pictures into a book.
I am taking the book to school for Show and Tell.

Number of words	**40**
	_____
	- - - - - - - - -
My best time	_____
	_____
	- - - - - - - - -
Words per minute	_____

© Harcourt

LA.A.1.1.4(1.1) uses a variety of strategies to comprehend text (for example, retelling stories in correct sequence, recalling details, rereading).
LA.A.2.1.2(1.2) reads aloud familiar stories, poems, or passages with a beginning degree of fluency and expression.

Lesson 5: Trading Goods and Services

Building Vocabulary

Read the sentence below. Then draw a line to match the picture of the goods to the stores where you would buy them.

Goods are things that people make to sell or trade.

Goods	Stores
food	book store
pets	grocery store
toys	toy store
books	pet shop

LA.A.1.1.2(1.5) uses context clues to construct meaning (meaning cues) (for example, illustrations, knowledge of the story and topic).
LA.A.1.1.3(1.3) uses resources and references (for example, illustrations, knowledge of the story and topic) beginning dictionaries, available technology to build upon word meanings.

Reading Support for Social Studies

Name _____ Date _____

Reading Primary Sources

The way people travel has changed over many years. Look at the photograph and its caption. Then answer the questions.

1 Was this photograph taken today or a long time ago? How can you tell?

_____

- -

_____

_____

- -

_____

_____

- -

_____

(continued)

© Harcourt

LA.A.2.1.1(1.1) knows the main idea or theme and supporting details of a story or informational piece.
LA.A.2.1.1(1.2) uses specific details and information from a text to answer literal questions.

2 Does this picture show travel on land, on water, or in the air?

_____

- -

_____

3 Circle the horse and buggy in the photograph. Would you like to travel this way? Write a sentence telling why.

_____

- -

_____

- -

_____

4 What ways have you traveled before? Which way do you like the best?

_____

- -

_____

_____

- -

_____

_____

- -

_____

_____

- -

_____

LA.A.2.1.1(1.1) knows the main idea or theme and supporting details of a story or informational piece.
LA.A.2.1.1(1.2) uses specific details and information from a text to answer literal questions.

FCAT Test Prep

Read the passage "Henry Flagler and Florida's Tourist Business" before answering Numbers 1 through 5. Circle the letter of the best answer.

Henry Flagler and Florida's Tourist Business

Henry Flagler was a business leader in New York City. One winter, he visited St. Augustine, Florida. He saw that the warm weather could bring tourists from the North. He decided to build hotels along the east coast of Florida.

Henry Flagler also built a railway in Florida. It let visitors travel by train from Jacksonville to Miami. He worked to make Miami a good place to visit. He built streets and provided water and electricity. Henry Flagler started the tourist business that is so important to Florida today.

Go On ▶

Now answer Numbers 1 through 5. Base your answers on the passage "Henry Flagler and Florida's Tourist Business."

1 **Henry Flagler lived in**

A   Atlanta.

B   New York City.

C   Buffalo.

D   Cleveland.

2 **Why did Henry Flagler think tourists would like Florida?**

F   It had warm weather.

G   It was pretty.

H   It was near the ocean.

I   It was sunny.

3 **Visitors could ride Henry Flagler's railway from Jacksonville to**

A   St. Augustine.

B   New York City.

C   Miami.

D   Tampa.

4 **What did Henry Flagler NOT do in Miami?**

F   He built streets.

G   He provided water.

H   He provided electricity.

I   He built hotels.

5 **Write a sentence that describes what Henry Flagler did.**

READ
THINK
EXPLAIN

_____

_ _

_____

_ _

_____

STOP

Focus Skill Categorize

When you categorize things, you group them. Read the list. Group the words in the correct boxes.

lake, hill, plain, house, school, river

REMEMBER

• Group words for land, water, and buildings in the boxes.

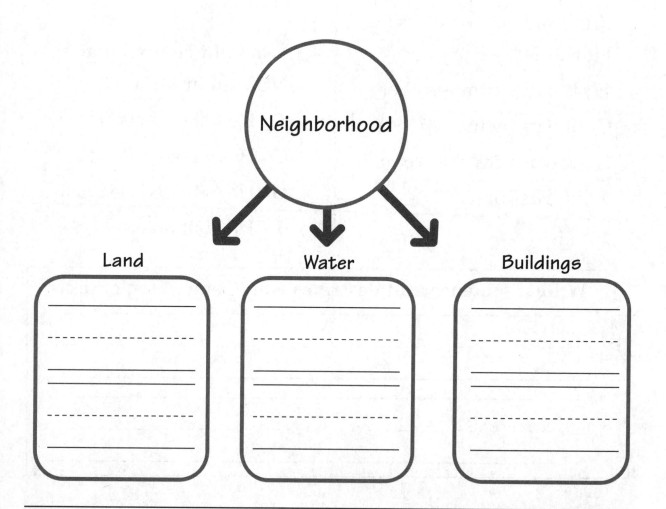

LA.A.1.1.4(1.1) uses a variety of strategies to comprehend text (for example, retelling stories in correct sequence, recalling details, rereading).
LA.A.2.1.3(1.1) reads for information used in performing tasks (for example, directions, graphs, charts, signs, captions).

Name _____ Date _____

Building Text Comprehension
Categorize

Read the paragraph. As you read, think about your neighborhood. Think about places you would show to a new neighbor. Then fill in the chart on the next page.

Tony moved to a new neighborhood. He and his dad took a bicycle ride on Sunday. They saw many trees during their ride. Tony saw that his new school was near a mountain. The grocery store was just around the corner by the river. The library was on the same street as the bank. Tony could see a hill just past the lake. He saw many fish in the lake. After the bike ride, Tony knew his way around his new neighborhood.

(continued)

LA.A.1.1.4(1.1) uses a variety of strategies to comprehend text (for example, retelling stories in correct sequence, recalling details, rereading).
LA.A.2.1.3(1.1) reads for information used in performing tasks (for example, directions, graphs, charts, signs, captions).

Name _____ Date _____

Fill in the chart.

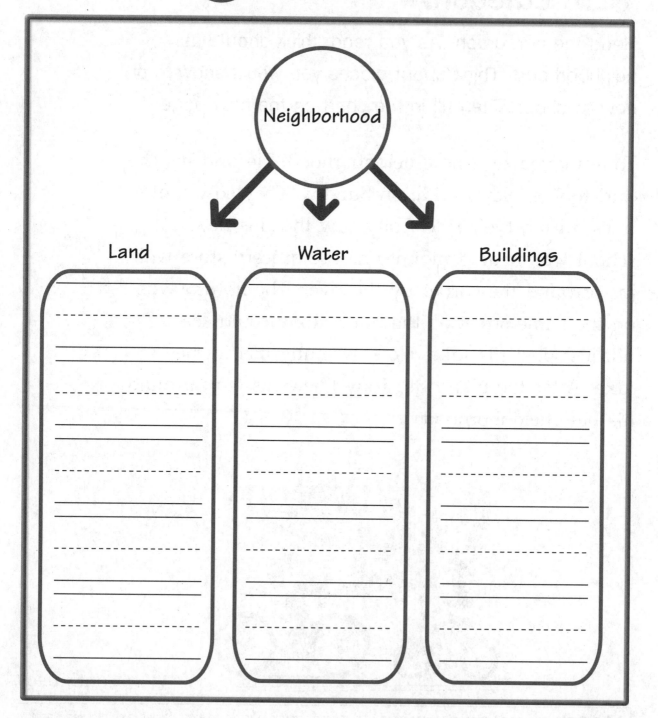

LA.A.2.1.3(1.1) reads for information used in performing tasks (for example, directions, graphs, charts, signs, captions).

Lesson 2: Our Treasured Resources

Building Fluency

Part A. Practice reading the words aloud.

Vocabulary Words	Additional Words
resource	gasoline
forest	soil
farm	

Part B. First, practice reading aloud the phrases. Then, practice reading aloud the sentences.

1 A resource / is something / we need.

2 Many trees grow / in a forest.

3 Cars need gasoline / to run.

4 Trees and plants / grow in soil.

5 A farm helps / us meet / our needs.

(continued)

LA.A.1.1.4(1.1) uses a variety of strategies to comprehend text (for example, retelling stories in correct sequence, recalling details, rereading).
LA.A.2.1.2(1.2) reads aloud familiar stories, poems, or passages with a beginning degree of fluency and expression.

Use with Unit 4, Lesson 2.   37   **Reading Support for Social Studies**

© Harcourt

Part C. Read aloud the passage below three times. Try to improve your reading each time. Record your best time on the lines below.

Soil is very important to farms. A farm is land that is used to grow plants and raise animals. The plants and animals help us meet our needs for food and clothing.

Number of words	**32**
	_____
	- - - - - - - - -
My best time	_____
	_____
	- - - - - - - - -
Words per minute	_____

LA.A.1.1.4(1.1) uses a variety of strategies to comprehend text (for example, retelling stories in correct sequence, recalling details, rereading).
LA.A.2.1.2(1.2) reads aloud familiar stories, poems, or passages with a beginning degree of fluency and expression.

© Harcourt

Name _____ Date _____

Reading Biographies

Read the paragraphs. Then write a sentence. Tell how
Gutzon Borglum is an example of the character trait
responsibility.

Gutzon Borglum
Character Trait: Responsibility

Gutzon Borglum carved
the heads of four American
presidents into Mt. Rushmore.
Mt. Rushmore is a mountain
in South Dakota. About 400
people helped to work on
the sculpture.

Borglum and his workers used dynamite to blast out
large pieces of stone. Then they carved faces of George
Washington, Thomas Jefferson, Theodore Roosevelt,
and Abraham Lincoln. Borglum worked for fourteen
years on his sculpture. Today his art is known as
Mt. Rushmore National Monument.

_____

- -

_____

LA.A.2.1.1(1.1) knows the main idea or theme and supporting details of a story or informational piece.
LA.A.2.1.1(1.3) makes inferences based on text and prior knowledge (for example, regarding a character's traits,
feelings, or actions).

Lesson 4: The Cheese Factory

Building Vocabulary

Read the following paragraph. Define the word <u>factory</u> using clues from the paragraph.

Mrs. Karl's class visited a <u>factory</u>. The <u>factory</u> made cheese from milk. When the cheese is made, trucks carry the product to stores. At the store, Mrs. Karl's class can purchase the cheese that was made in the <u>factory</u>.

A <u>factory</u> is

_____

- -

_____

Now, draw a picture of two products that you think are made in a <u>factory</u> .

LA.A.1.1.2(1.5) use context clues to construct meaning (meaning cues) (for example, illustrations, knowledge of the story and topic).
LA.A.1.1.3(1.3) uses resources and references (for example, illustrations, knowledge of the story and topic) beginning dictionaries, available technology to build upon word meanings.

© Harcourt

Name _____ Date _____

Reading Biographies

Read the paragraph. Then complete the sections below and on the next page.

Marjory Stoneman Douglas
Character Trait: Citizenship

Marjory Stoneman Douglas worried about Florida's natural resources. Many people thought the Everglades in south Florida was just another swamp. Marjory Stoneman Douglas knew it was a huge, slow-moving river. For more than 25 years, she worked to protect the plants and animals that live there.

Write a sentence about how Marjory Stoneman Douglas shows the character trait **citizenship**.

_____

- -

_____

_____

- -

_____

(continued)

LA.A.2.1.1(1.2) uses specific details and information from a text to answer literal questions.
LA.A.2.1.1(1.3) makes references based on text and prior knowledge (for example, regarding a character's traits, feelings, or actions).

© Harcourt

Name _____ Date _____

Make a poster asking people to protect the Everglades.
Draw a picture and write words that will show how
important the environment is to all of us.

LA.A.2.1.1(1.3) makes inferences based on text and prior knowledge (for example, regarding a character's traits, feelings, or actions).
LA.D.2.1.1(1.1) understands that word choice can shape ideas, feelings, and actions (for example, multiple meaning words, figurative language).

FCAT Test Prep

Read the passage "Presidential Election" before answering Numbers 1 through 5. Circle the letter of the best answer.

Presidential Election

Every four years the American people vote for a President. Two main candidates ran for President in 2004. A candidate is someone who hopes to be elected for a job. President

George W. Bush

George W. Bush was one of the candidates. The other candidate was a Senator from Massachusetts named John Kerry. Millions of people voted on Election Day. Many stood in long lines for hours. Some were young people who had never voted before. Others were voting for the first time in many years. Everyone knew that his or her vote counted. The American people decided to keep George W. Bush as their President for another four years.

Go On ▶

© Harcourt

Now answer Numbers 1 through 5. Base your answers on the passage "Presidential Election."

1 The American people vote for a President every

A   three years.

B   four years.

C   five years.

D   six years.

2 A candidate is someone who

F   votes for President.

G   works for the President.

H   hopes to be elected for a job.

I   makes laws.

3 How many people voted on Election Day?

A   hundreds

B   thousands

C   millions

D   billions

4 Who won the Presidential election of 2004?

F   Bill Clinton

G   John Kerry

H   George W. Bush

I   Ronald Reagan

5 Write a sentence that tells the most interesting thing you learned about the Presidential election of 2004.

READ
THINK
EXPLAIN

_____

_____

_____

STOP

© Harcourt

Summarize

Read the paragraph. Then fill in the diagram.

The state of Florida has many symbols. A symbol is an object that stands for something else. Florida's state flower is the orange blossom. Farms in Florida produce more than half of all the oranges sold in the United States. Florida also has a state reptile, the alligator. Alligators are common in Florida.

REMEMBER

- Main ideas show you what you are reading about.
- Use the main ideas to summarize what you learned.

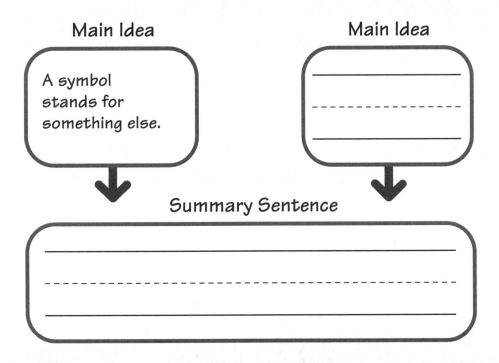

Main Idea

A symbol stands for something else.

Main Idea

Summary Sentence

LA.A.2.1.1(1.1) knows the main idea or theme and supporting details of a story or informational piece.
LA.A.2.1.3(1.1) reads for information used in performing tasks (for example, directions, graphs, charts, signs, captions).

Lesson 1: Sharing the Land

Building Text Comprehension
Summarize

Read the story. Look for the main ideas. Then complete the diagram on the next page.

Florida has not always been part of the United States. Many years ago, only Native Americans lived in what is now Florida. Later, explorers from Europe settled in Florida.

At one time, Spain claimed Florida. Spanish settlers built a large fort at St. Augustine. French settlers also said that Florida was theirs. The Spanish and French fought many battles. Then England claimed Florida. They ruled the area for many years.

In 1845 Florida became the 27th state of the United States. Today people in Florida are part of the United States. Many tourists, or visitors, come to Florida. Some of these tourists come from England, France, and Spain.

(continued)

LA.A.2.1.1(1.1) knows the main idea or theme and supporting details of a story or informational piece.
LA.A.2.1.3(1.1) reads for information used in performing tasks (for example, directions, graphs, charts, signs, captions).

Fill in the diagram.

⭐ Focus Skill Summarize

Main Idea	Main Idea	Main Idea

Summary Sentence

_____

LA.A.2.1.1(1.1) knows the main idea or theme and supporting details of a story or informational piece.
LA.A.2.1.3(1.1) reads for information used in performing tasks (for example, directions, graphs, charts, signs, captions).

Name _____ Date _____

Reading Biographies

Read the paragraph. Then write a sentence about how
Pedro Menéndez de Avilés shows the character trait
patriotism.

Pedro Menéndez de Avilés
Character Trait: Patriotism

Pedro Menéndez de Avilés was born in
Avilés, Spain, in 1519. When he grew
up, he became an explorer for the
Spanish king. In 1565 King Philip II
of Spain paid Menéndez to start a
settlement in Florida. Menéndez
named the settlement St. Augustine.
St. Augustine became the first long-
lasting settlement in the United States.
Menéndez was the governor of Florida
until he died in 1574.

_____

- -

_____

- -

_____

- -

_____

LA.A.2.1.1(1.2) uses specific details and information from a text to answer literal questions.
LA.A.2.1.1(1.3) makes inferences based on text and prior knowledge (for example, regarding a character's traits, feelings, or actions).

© Harcourt

Name _____ Date _____

Building Vocabulary

Read the following paragraph. Think about the meaning of the underlined words.

America's Independence

America celebrates its <u>history</u> on July 4. On that day in 1776, America became free. But it was not easy. Americans had to fight for their rights. General George Washington became a <u>hero</u> in American <u>history</u>. After America won their independence, George Washington was elected <u>President</u> of our country. He was the first <u>President</u> of the United States of America.

Use what you learned about America's independence to fill in the blanks below.

_____

- -

A part of American _____ is the story of George Washington. During the war for independence, he

_____

- -

became a _____ by helping our country

_____

- -

gain its freedom. He was the first _____ of the United States of America.

LA.A.1.1.2(1.5) uses context clues to construct meaning (meaning cues) (for example, illustrations, knowledge of the story and topic).
LA.A.1.1.3(1.3) uses resources and references (for example, illustrations, knowledge of the story and topic) beginning dictionaries, available technology to build upon word meanings.

Lesson 4: "America the Beautiful"

Building Fluency

Part A. Practice reading the words aloud.

Vocabulary Words
spacious
amber
majesties
brotherhood

Part B. First, practice reading aloud the phrases. Then, practice reading aloud the sentences.

1 The skies / are big / and spacious.

2 Amber waves of grain / celebrates America's farms.

3 Purple mountain majesties / are a part / of America's land.

4 We live / in a brotherhood.

(continued)

LA.A.1.1.4(1.1) uses a variety of strategies to comprehend text (for example, retelling stories in correct sequence, recalling details, rereading).
LA.A.2.1.2(1.2) reads aloud familiar stories, poems, or passages with a beginning degree of fluency and expression.

© Harcourt

Name _____ Date _____

Part C. The passage below is from "America the Beautiful" by Katharine Lee Bates. Read aloud the passage three times. Try to improve your reading each time. Record your best time on the lines below.

O beautiful for spacious skies,

For amber waves of grain,

For purple mountain majesties

Above the fruited plain!

America! America!

God shed His grace on thee

And crown thy good with brotherhood

From sea to shining sea!

Number of words		37
		_____
		- - - - - - - - -
My best time		_____
		_____
		- - - - - - - - -
Words per minute		_____

LA.A.1.1.4(1.1) uses a variety of strategies to comprehend text (for example, retelling stories in correct sequence, recalling details, rereading).
LA.A.2.1.2(1.2) reads aloud familiar stories, poems, or passages with a beginning degree of fluency and expression.

FCAT Test Prep

Read the passage "Hurricanes" before answering
Numbers 1 through 5. Circle the letter of the best
answer.

Hurricanes

June to November of each year is hurricane
season. Hurricanes are storms with strong winds
and heavy rains. A hurricane begins over warm
ocean waters. Its winds become stronger as the
storm travels over the ocean. When hurricanes hit
land they cause a lot of damage. Four hurricanes
hit Florida in August and September of 2004. They
were named Hurricane Charley, Hurricane
Frances, Hurricane Ivan, and Hurricane Jeanne.
The rain and winds from the hurricanes damaged
many homes and businesses in Florida.

Go On ▶

© Harcourt

Now answer Numbers 1 through 5. Base your answers on the passage "Hurricanes."

1 **Hurricane season is from**

   A November to December.

   B June to November.

   C April to June.

   D December to June.

2 **A hurricane is a storm with**

   F snow and ice.

   G heat and dust.

   H wind and rain.

   I hail and sleet.

3 **How many hurricanes hit Florida in 2004?**

   A three

   B one

   C five

   D four

4 **What were the names of the hurricanes?**

   F Andrew, Gina, Scott, Paula

   G Charley, Frances, Ivan, and Jeanne

   H Martha, Leo, Nick, and Heather

   I Tom, Sarah, Jill, and John

5 **Write a sentence that tells about the damage a hurricane can cause.**

READ
THINK
EXPLAIN

_____

_____

_____

_____

_____

© Harcourt

Focus Skill **Generalize**

Read the paragraph. Find the facts. Then write the big idea.

Our world is on a planet named Earth. We live on a continent, or a large piece of land on Earth that lies between two oceans. At the very bottom of the world is a continent called Antarctica. It is small in size compared to the continent we live on. Antarctica is the coldest and windiest continent in the world. It also has the least amount of people living there. The land of Antarctica is covered with a sheet of ice that is one-mile-thick.

REMEMBER

- Facts are statements that are true.
- Use all the facts to identify the big idea.

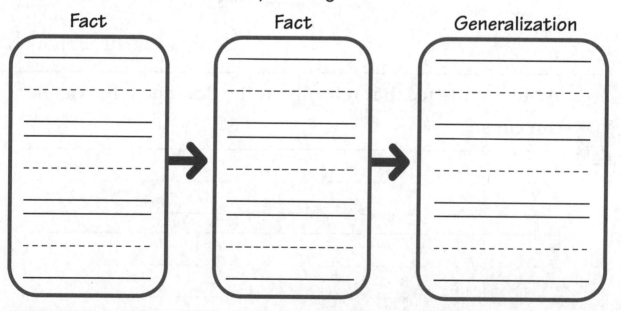

Fact → Fact → Generalization

LA.A.2.1.1(1.1) knows the main idea or theme and supporting details of a story or informational piece.
LA.A.2.1.3(1.1) reads for information used in performing tasks (for example, directions, graphs, charts, signs, captions).

© Harcourt

Lesson 1: Where in the World Do People Live?

Building Text Comprehension
Generalize

Read the paragraphs. As you read, find facts that prove a big idea. Then fill in the diagram on the next page.

Korea is an Asian country. In Korea, it is not polite to call someone by his or her first name. You should first use a proper title, such as Mr., Mrs., or Miss. Teachers and doctors are spoken to by naming their position first. Then you add the last name, or family name. Koreans follow this custom to show their respect for others.

Another Korean custom is to give a gift when you meet someone. A gift shows that you are interested in that person. However, it is not polite to open the gift in front of the person who gave it. Wrapped gifts are not opened when others are around. The Korean people have a respectful culture.

(continued)

LA.A.1.1.4(1.1) uses a variety of strategies to comprehend text (for example, retelling stories in correct sequence, recalling details, rereading).
LA.A.2.1.3(1.1) reads for information used in performing tasks (for example, directions, graphs, charts, signs, captions).

Name _____ Date _____

Complete the diagram.

 **Generalize**

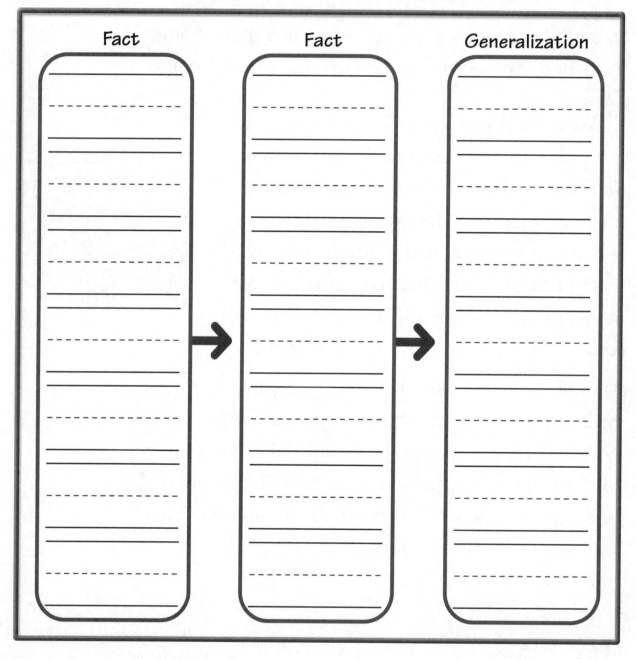

Fact   Fact   Generalization

LA.A.2.1.1(1.1) knows the main idea or theme and supporting details of a story or informational piece.
LA.A.2.1.3(1.1) reads for information used in performing tasks (for example, directions, graphs, charts, signs, captions).

© Harcourt

Lesson 2: People Are People Everywhere

Using Charts and Graphs

Look at the chart of Australian words and their English meanings. Then answer the questions below.

English Meaning	Australian Meaning
chicken	chook
friend	mate
candy	lollies
farmhand (helper)	jackaroo
hello	g'day

1 What is the Australian word for friend?

_____

- -

_____

2 If someone asked for some lollies, what would they be asking for?

_____

- -

_____

3 When would someone say "g'day" to you?

_____

- -

_____

LA.A.2.1.5(1.1) uses simple reference material to obtain information (for example, table of contents, fiction and nonfiction books, picture dictionaries, audio visual software).

Lesson 3: "The Mouse in the Chest"

Building Fluency

Part A. Practice reading the words aloud.

Vocabulary Words
chest lid beautiful silly

Part B. First, practice reading aloud the phrases. Then, practice reading aloud the sentences.

1 All of her life, / the mouse lived in the chest.

2 When the lid / of the chest / was open, / the mouse got out.

3 Outside, the mouse / saw that the world / was a beautiful place.

4 The mouse saw / that she was silly, / because she never left / her home.

(continued)

LA.A.1.1.4(1.1) uses a variety of strategies to comprehend text (for example, retelling stories in correct sequence, recalling details, rereading).
LA.A.2.1.2(1.2) reads aloud familiar stories, poems, or passages with a beginning degree of fluency and expression.

© Harcourt

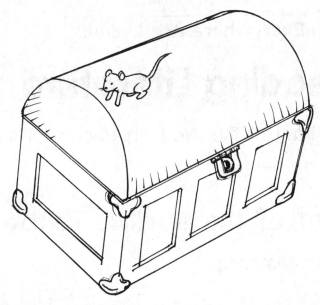

Part C. The passage below is from "The Mouse in the Chest" by Aesop. Read aloud the passage three times. Try to improve your reading each time. Record your best time on the lines below.

A mouse had lived all her life in a chest. She ate only the food she found there. The mouse was very happy in the chest. She never wanted to get out.

Number of words	32
My best time	
Words per minute	

(continued)

LA.A.1.1.4(1.1) uses a variety of strategies to comprehend text (for example, retelling stories in correct sequence, recalling details, rereading).
LA.A.2.1.2(1.2) reads aloud familiar stories, poems, or passages with a beginning degree of fluency and expression.

Name _____ Date _____

Reading Literature

Read the poem "Chant of the Working People." Then answer the questions below.

Chant of the Working People

When the sun comes up

I set out

for the factory,

when the sun comes up,

for I am the laborer,

I am the worker,

when the sun comes up.

1 What does the worker do?

_____

- -

_____

2 What kinds of things do you think are made in factories?

_____

- -

_____

© Harcourt

LA.A.2.1.1(1.1) knows the main idea or theme and supporting details of a story or informational piece.
LA.A.2.1.1(1.2) uses specific details and information from a text to answer literal questions.

Lesson 5: People Talk Around the World

Building Vocabulary

Look at the pictures on this page and the next page.
Think of other ways people share ideas. Then answer
the questions about **communication.**

❶ What are two ways people send messages?

_____

- -

_____

❷ Which came first, the telephone or the computer?

_____

- -

_____

(continued)

LA.A.1.1.3(1.3) uses resources and references (for example, illustrations, knowledge of the story and topic) beginning dictionaries, available technology to build upon word meanings.
LA.A.2.1.1(1.2) uses specific details and information from a text to answer literal questions.

Name _____ Date _____

3 What can you do on a computer that you cannot do on a telephone?

_____

- -

_____

4 Draw a picture of your favorite way to send a message.

LA.A.1.1.3(1.3) uses resources and references (for example, illustrations, knowledge of the story and topic) beginning dictionaries, available technology to build upon word meanings.
LA.A.2.1.1(1.2) uses specific details and information from a text to answer literal questions.

Reading Support for Social Studies   62   Use with Unit 6, Lesson 5.

Name _____ Date _____

Reading Biographies

Read the paragraphs. Then answer the questions about Jane Goodall.

Jane Goodall
Character Trait: Respect

On Jane Goodall's second birthday, her father gave her a toy chimpanzee. She named it Jubilee. Jane learned all she could about chimps and other animals. Jane made her first trip to Kenya, Africa, when she was 23. At first, she worked in a museum.

Later Jane Goodall studied the chimpanzees of Gombe. She went to their habitat, or the area where they lived. In the beginning, the chimps would run from her. After several months, they became used to having her around.

(continued)

LA.A.2.1.1(1.1) knows the main idea or theme and supporting details of a story or informational piece.
LA.A.2.1.3(1.1) reads for information used in performing tasks (for example, directions, graphs, charts, signs, captions).

Jane Goodall discovered that chimpanzees are very smart. Chimpanzees make and use tools. They hunt and eat meat. Through her work, Jane Goodall teaches us to take care of the place where we live. This idea is important for all living things.

1 Name two animals that share our planet with us.

_____

- -

_____

- -

_____

2 How is Jane Goodall an example of the character trait respect?

CHARACTER EDUCATION

_____

- -

_____

_____

- -

_____

LA.A.2.1.1(1.2) uses specific details and information from a text to answer literal questions.
LA.A.2.1.1(1.3) makes inferences based on text and prior knowledge (for example, regarding a character's traits, feelings, or actions).
LA.A.2.1.3(1.1) reads for information used in performing tasks (for example, directions, graphs, charts, signs, captions).

FCAT Test Prep

Read the passage "The Land Down Under" before answering Numbers 1 through 5. Circle the letter of the best answer.

The Land Down Under

Australia is both a continent and a country. It is about the size of the United States. Most people in Australia live in or near cities, and they speak English.

Australia is called "the land down under" because it lies south of the equator. Because of its location, Australia has winter when we have summer.

A large part of the country is called the outback. Very few people live in this region. Some sheep and cattle ranches are located in the outback. Children who live on these ranches have to use radios to listen to their school lessons.

Go On ▶

65

Reading Support for Social Studies

1 **Australia is both**

   A a state and a territory.

   B a continent and a country.

   C a city and a continent.

   D a country and a state.

2 **What language do people in Australia speak?**

   F English

   G Australian

   H French

   I Outback

3 **Australia and the United States are**

   A continents.

   B about the same size.

   C warm during July.

   D not alike in any way.

4 **How do children on ranches learn?**

   F They attend school.

   G They are taught at home by their parents.

   H They do not learn.

   I They listen to their lessons on radios.

---

5 **List two ways Australia and the United States are different.**

READ
THINK
EXPLAIN

_____

- -

_____

- -

_____

© Harcourt

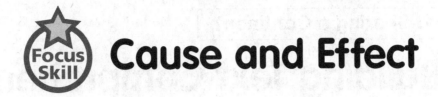

Cause and Effect

Read the paragraph. Then fill in the diagram.

Long ago, the rulers of China built the longest wall in the world. Each leader added to the wall. Armies protected the wall. The wall protected the rulers' land. The wall stretched over mountains for more than 4,000 miles. Today, large sections of the wall are in ruins. People from around the world often visit the parts that remain.

REMEMBER

- To find the effect, ask "What happened?"
- To find the cause, ask "Why did it happen?"

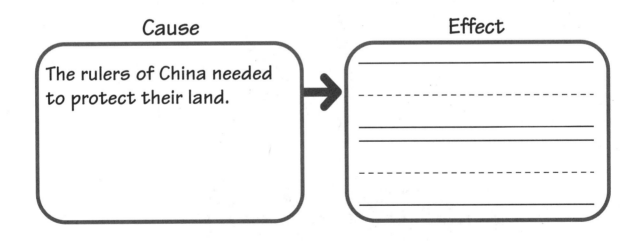

Cause

The rulers of China needed to protect their land.

Effect

LA.A.2.1.1(1.1) knows the main idea or theme and supporting details of a story or informational piece.
LA.A.2.1.3(1.1) reads for information used in performing tasks (for example, directions, graphs, charts, signs, captions).

© Harcourt

Lesson 1: Sharing a Continent

Building Text Comprehension
Cause and Effect

Read the paragraph. As you read think about the causes and effects of volcanoes. Then fill in the diagram on the next page.

There are many volcanoes in Mexico. El Chichon is a mountain that is also a volcano. It erupted, or exploded, in 1982. When El Chichon erupted, it destroyed villages and crops. A hole was left at the top of the mountain. It is very deep and wide. Today there is a lake filling that hole. You cannot swim in this lake. The water is very hot and filled with poisonous acids and gases.

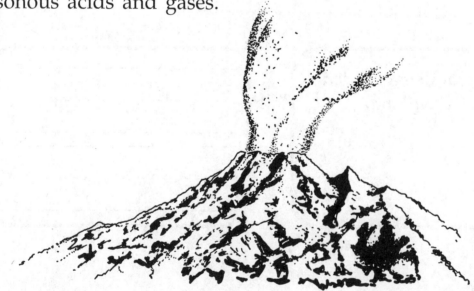

(continued)

LA.A.1.1.4(1.1) uses a variety of strategies to comprehend text (for example, retelling stories in correct sequence, recalling details, rereading).
LA.A.2.1.3(1.1) reads for information used in performing tasks (for example, directions, graphs, charts, signs, captions).

Fill in the diagram.

Focus Skill — Cause and Effect

Cause	Effect

LA.A.2.1.3(1.1) reads for information used in performing tasks (for example, directions, graphs, charts, signs, captions).

Lesson 2: People on Other Continents

Reading Maps and Globes

Find the seven continents on this map. Then answer the questions.

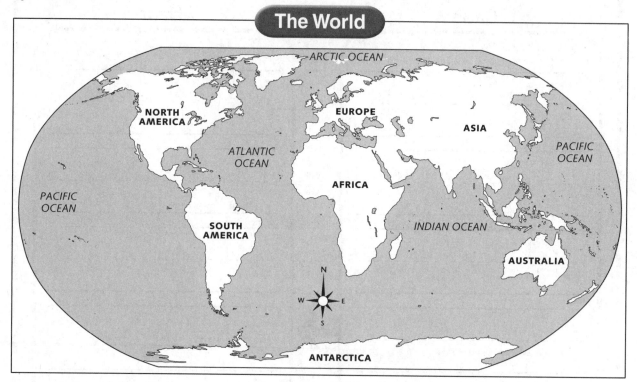

The World

1 Mark an X on the continent where Egypt is found.

2 Find the correct continent for Brazil. Color that continent red.

3 Circle the southernmost continent.

4 Color the continent that is also a country.

5 Look at page 207 in your textbook. Color Europe yellow, and color Asia orange.

6 Circle the continent where you live.

LA.A.2.1.5(1.1) uses simple reference material to obtain information (for example, table of contents, fiction and nonfiction books, picture dictionaries, audio visual software).

© Harcourt

Name _____ Date _____

Building Fluency

Part A. Practice reading the words aloud.

Vocabulary Words
folktale
umbrellas
worried
straw shoes

Part B. First, practice reading aloud the phrases.

Then, practice reading aloud the sentences.

1 This story / is a Korean folktale.

2 The mother worried / about her sons.

3 The rain caused / one son / to sell his umbrellas.

4 The rain caused / the other son / to not sell his straw shoes.

(continued)

LA.A.1.1.4(1.1) uses a variety of strategies to comprehend text (for example, retelling stories in correct sequence, recalling details, rereading).
LA.A.2.1.2(1.2) reads aloud familiar stories, poems, or passages with a beginning degree of fluency and expression.

Name _____ Date _____

Part C. The passage below is from the Korean folktale "Umbrellas and Straw Shoes." Read aloud the passage three times. Try to improve your reading each time. Record your best time on the lines below.

The woman was always worried and never happy. Then a friend pointed out to her that whatever the weather, one son would always be selling his goods. The woman had to agree! After she learned to look on the bright side of things, she was happy all the time.

Number of words	49
My best time	
Words per minute	

LA.A.1.1.4(1.1) uses a variety of strategies to comprehend text (for example, retelling stories in correct sequence, recalling details, rereading).
LA.A.2.1.2(1.2) reads aloud familiar stories, poems, or passages with a beginning degree of fluency and expression.

© Harcourt

| Lesson 4: People in Different Times |

Reading Biographies

Read the paragraphs. Then write a sentence. Tell how Frida Kahlo is an example of the character trait **patriotism**.

Frida Kahlo
Character Trait: Patriotism

Frida Kahlo was born in Mexico. When Frida was 15 years old, she was badly hurt in a bus accident. She spent a lot of time in bed getting better. During that time, Frida taught herself how to paint.

Frida's paintings showed that she was proud of her country's history. She often painted times in Mexican history. Many of Frida's paintings were also self-portraits. She painted herself wearing colorful Mexican costumes.

_____

- -

_____

_____

- -

_____

LA.A.2.1.1(1.2) uses specific details and information from a text to answer literal questions.
LA.A.2.1.1(1.3) makes inferences based on text and prior knowledge (for example, regarding a character's traits, feelings, or actions).

Lesson 5: People Share Their History

Reading Primary Sources

Look at the picture. It shows a totem pole made by the Florida Native Americans called the Timucuas. Then answer the questions.

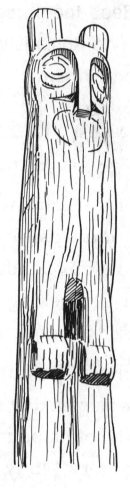

1 Why do you think the Timucuas chose to sculpt the horned owl?

_____

- -

_____

- -

_____

2 What can we learn about the Timucuas by looking at this totem pole?

_____

- -

_____

_____

- -

_____

LA.A.1.1.4(1.1) uses a variety of strategies to comprehend text (for example, retelling stories in correct sequence, recalling details, rereading).
LA.A.2.1.1(1.1) knows the main idea or theme and supporting details of a story or informational piece.

Lesson 6: Postcards from America

Building Vocabulary

An inverter is someone who thinks of or makes something for the first time. Below is a list of inventors and their inventions. Use what you learned in Lesson 6. Write the inventors in the left column and their inventions in the right column.

Orville and Wilbur Wright

lightbulb

airplane

Lewis Latimer

Inventors	Inventions

LA.A.1.1.2(1.5) uses context clues to construct meaning (meaning cues) (for example, illustrations, knowledge of the story and topic).
LA.A.1.1.3(1.3) uses resources and references (for example, illustrations, knowledge of the story and topic) beginning dictionaries, available technology to build upon word meanings.

FCAT Test Prep

Read the passage "The Statue of Liberty" before answering Numbers 1 through 5. Circle the letter of the best answer.

The Statue of Liberty

The Statue of Liberty was built in France as a gift to the United States. Then it was taken apart and sent to the United States. The statue arrived in New York in 350 pieces. It took Americans four months to put the pieces back together. On a fall day in 1886, the United States thanked France for the giant gift at a celebration.

Today, anyone can visit the statue on Liberty Island. It is as tall as a 30-story building. Visitors can climb steps almost to her crown. From there they can look out over New York City.

Go On ▶

Now answer Numbers 1 through 5. Base your answers
on the passage "The Statue of Liberty."

1 **Which happened FIRST?**

   A The statue arrived in
New York in pieces.

   B The Statue of Liberty
was built in France.

   C It took four months to
put it together.

   D It was taken apart.

2 **Before the statue was sent
to the United States, it**

   F was taken apart.

   G arrived in New York.

   H was accepted at a
celebration.

   I was put together.

3 **Where is the Statue of
Liberty today?**

   A Florida

   B Liberty Island

   C France

   D Washington, D.C.

4 **Which happened LAST?**

   F Americans put the
statue back together.

   G The French took the
statue apart.

   H The United States
thanked France.

   I The statue was made.

5 **READ THINK EXPLAIN** **Imagine that you are visiting the Statue of Liberty. Write
a list of words that describe the statue.**

_____

_____

_____

_____

_____

© Harcourt